Two's Company

by Shirley Greenway

Photographs by Oxford Scientific Films

HOUGHTON MIFFLIN
BOSTON • MORRIS PLAINS, NJ

California • Colorado • Georgia • Illinois • New Jersey • Texas

To Mattachin and Hiroshige – two's company . . . S.G.

TWO'S COMPANY, by Shirley Greenway, photographs by Oxford Scientific Films. Text copyright © 1997 by Shirley Greenway. Photographs © 1997 by Oxford Scientific Films (and individual copyright holders). Created by White Cottage Children's Books, London, England. Reprinted by arrangement with Charlesbridge Publishing, Watertown, MA.

Photographer Credits: **Title Page** Steve Turner; **Introduction** Rudie Kuiter; 4–5 (tl) John Downer; (m) (r) Hans Reinhard/Okapia; 6–7 Tom McHugh/Photo Researchers; 8 (tl) Konrad Wothe; (r) Daniel J. Cox; 9 (r) G.A. Maclean; 10 (l) Alain Christof; (m) (tr) David Thompson; 11 Phil Devries; 12 Bruce Davidson; 13 Anthony Bannister; 14–15 (tl) John Gerlach/Animals Animals; (bl) Michael W. Richards; (r) Miriam Austerman; 16–17 Howard Hall; 18 (tl) Daniel J. Cox; (r) Frank Schneidermeyer; 19 Michael Fogden; 20 (tl) Hans & Judy Beste; (r) Des & Jen Bartlett/Survival; 21 Kathie Atkinson; 22–23 G.I. Bernard; 24–25 (l) (t) Mickey Gibson/Animals Animals; (r) David Shale/Survival; 26 (tl) William Bacon/Photo Researchers; (r) Jeff Lepore/Photo Researchers; 27 Lon Lauker; 28 (tl) Steve Turner (r) William Paton/Survival; 29 Des & Jen Bartlett/Survival; 30 Dr. A.C. Twomey/Photo Researchers; 31 (l) Frank Schneidermeyer; (r) Tom McHugh/Photo Researchers.

Houghton Mifflin Edition, 2005
Copyright © 2001 by Houghton Mifflin Company. All rights reserved.

Printed in the U.S.A.

ISBN 0-618-06701-9
56789-B-05 04

Some animals live alone,
some live in families,
and some live in groups,
each with its own special name.
   Two is company, but three
can be a flock or a herd,
a school or a pod . . .

One sheep alone,
two sheep together —

a flock of sheep
grazing in the snow.

One small fish,
two shimmering fish —

a **shoal** of
silvery fish swimming.

One fox sniffing,
two foxes digging —

8

a **skulk** of foxes
hunting in the night.

One honeybee working,
two honeybees around
a flower —

a **swarm** of honeybees buzzing.

One zebra on the savanna,
two friendly zebras in
the bush —

a **herd** of zebras
gathered at the watering hole.

One goose floating,
two geese flying —

a **gaggle** of geese
rising into the sky.

One dolphin somersaulting
in the sea,
two dolphins swimming
together —

a **school** of dolphins gliding
through blue water.

One macaw all alone,
two macaws meeting —

a family of macaws
sitting on a wall.

One kangaroo hopping,
two kangaroos boxing —

a **troop** of kangaroos resting in the shade.

One mouse nibbling,
two mice kissing —

a **nest** of mice
hidden in the grass.

One stately camel,
two comical camels —

a **train** of camels traveling
across the sand.

One walrus showing
his fine tusks,
two walruses enjoying
a swim —

a **pod** of walruses sunbathing on the rocks.

One lazy lion yawning,
two contented lions resting —

a pride of lions drinking
in the afternoon.

So, whether you
belong to a family or a pair,
a group or a gathering,
a class or a crowd —

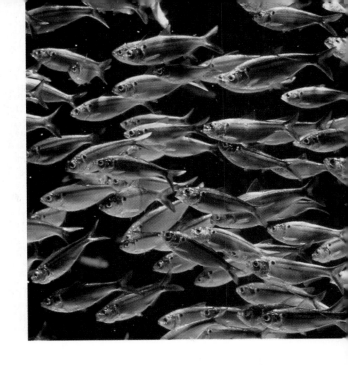

it's nice to be one,
and fun to be two,
but sometimes it's
good to be many!